STRAWBERRY MOON

RANDY MASCORRO

"Strawberry Moon"

I love you
And my
Mind
Is falling
And my
Heart
Is running
Your hands
Have a map
Stretching across them
Your lips
Are a light
I follow

Maybe water
Is what
I see
In you
How this
Is still
And frightening
How you are
Every shade
Of hope
How I am
Every troubled
Edge

I guess
It was the attraction
Of the way
You always
Balance me
How I am
Fast
And also
Unhurried
You pull me back
When I am full speed
And I notice
How you blink
And how your lips
Have so many
Stories
To tell me

I am
Tired
And in love
And my mind
Has been
Shaky
From the start
I miss
The ocean
But I see it
In your hair
Every day
You are
Saltwater
And sun

She'll lean back
And laugh
In a
Serious moment
Tales of sadness
Never looked
So good

I remember
Seeing you
Through the trees
The air
Was desire
And
The days
Were honey
I remember
How
The dandelions
Were blown
Away
When they
Saw you
Just like
I was

You are snow
Scattered across
The virginia hills
And the sunset
In colorado
Is painted on
Your lips
Those hands
They hold the new mexico
Desert
You are beauty
And you are
Everywhere

I love you
And
The days
Feel shorter
The rain
Falls harder
I never sleep
The nights
Are loud
Like my blood
When I see
You

Help me
Strip Away
What is keeping
Me hostage
My hands
Can't recognize
My skin anymore
And my voice
Is reckless
From the
Pain

I am hollow
I am fire
And I
Feel bloodless
But I love you

I love
You
In quiet
Moments
I love you
When my own
Silence
Is loud like
A bomb
I don't want
To balance
What I feel anymore
just let me
Collapse
And feel warmth
At the same
Time

I haven't made
Sense in awhile
This trial of fire
Is burning
Like a fence
In the middle
Of nowhere
If I am
Ashes
Your love
Will keep me
Sane
Baby, get your sea legs
Lets spend
Some time away

You hold
The earth
You're like
Sunlight
Through
The trees
I am water
With no direction
And my hands
Are cut
From swimming
Too freely

Her vibe
Fucked me
Differently
Every day
Nothing stood still
Those eyes
Were bright
Like city lights

Clear out
Time
Lets go watch
The strawberry moon shine
You and I
With all
The hours
In the
Sky
Lets forget
How it felt
When both of us
Were breathing hell
Lets go shine
Strawberry moon
Lets go shine

And i'll give you
The grains of my soul
We'll go and watch
The strawberry moon
We'll fade in the night
Dance under skies
I'll give you
The grains of my soul

I want you
In ways
That are not sane
And that's okay
Because a heart
Is meant
To beat wild
And my arms
Are torn
From loving
You
And letting
You go

The nights
Aren't
So quiet
Anymore
I hear your footsteps
They rattle
The floor
I am chased
By the hope
You have
In me

All the flowers
Are carried with you
Honey, all the good
Looks like you
When it rains
It pours
You got a storm
In that hair
Strike me
With lightning
Sweep me
Off
My feet

I love you
On land
I love you
In sea
My wounds heal up
From the way
Your name
Floats in
The air
Please listen
When I say
It is a good
Thing
To be tired
And awake

Let me tell
You
How my hands
Have always
Traced back
To yours
And what I feel
When I touch you
It's the
Summer solstice
And I am warm
Like
The path
Of the sun
In the sky

I am full
Of so many rocks
Heavy to touch
Strung out
On love
Swear if I know anything
It's that my life
Is in order
With your eyes
Beautiful
Stare me down
Dead

Even if
The sea
Went away
I would still
Feel it
From you
How your energy
Never settles
And how
My heart
Is always jumping
From the sight
Of you

I am
Ripped apart
But look at
All i've ever been
Flowers
In the palm
Of your
Hand

I spend time
Chasing shadows
But i've always
Wanted
To see behind walls
I felt her vibe
Like a drug
That hasn't been
Discovered yet
She pulls
The universe down
And I am covered
In constellations

I love
You
In colors
You are
This
Light show
That keeps me awake
I don't want to sleep
And see you
I am visible scars
And all I want
Is to
Heal
With my eyes
Open

Ocean goddess
With saltwater
In your hair
And those eyes
Are sparkling
Like the sun
At low tide

I'll rest
My head
For a few more hours
The evening
Wild
Like your legs
Those lips
Warm as
The sun

The city lights
Don't seem to sleep
Take this worry away from me
I hear your voice
And it keeps me home
I see your face
I'm not alone
Honey, there you are
With hope all in your hair
Honey, there you are
Dazzling as the stars

Days
Are falling
And I feel you
I love you in isolation
I hear you in this fire fight
That is taking over
The night
If I burn
What a pleasure it was
To see roses
Blooming
On a ruined
Wall

A lot of times
My own battles
Shake
And these roses
I carry
They fall
To pieces
As fast as I do
But always know
My attachment to you
Is written in
My bones

Whatever becomes
Of this
Always know
My time spent with you
Was heavier
Than gold
Being in your presence
Felt like I was
Being pulled by
The moon
And I am
Forever moved

Oh my heart
It's a rocket
And a bomb
Oh my soul
It's a race from afar
Time gets tangled
The pain never
Straightens
Oh my
Heart

It was like
Dipping my hands
In the ocean
She made me feel happy
And alive
Even with
All the
Mistakes on my back
Even with
All the debts
I carried around
On the soles
Of my feet

Sometimes
The meds
Make me slow down
But I always make sense
Of what you are
You are a million smiles
That burn in me
Like looking through
A kaleidoscope
You are every color
That changes
Constantly

How can I ever
Put into words
What she is?
She has
Given me
Endless sun
While I have emptied
My skeletons
At her feet

The mind
Wasn't so crippling
It was this paralyzing
Sea
That ran through me
I will love you
With nothing left
Sometimes getting
Out of bed
Felt like I
Was stepping on nails
I will love you
With nothing left

Touch me
As I am
Rugged
Barely holding on
I want you to kiss
The mistakes on my lips
I want to feel
My life fall
And rise
All at once

I began
To fall apart
Being light as a feather
Was a good thing
Whatever I was
A month ago
Let all that remains
Skin me clean
This troublesome life
Seems so achy as before
I'll walk through the shadows
I want my own mind
To love me more

Tired of
All the changing lights
Souls get rattled
We don't have to fly
Let's just stay here
Please hold me tight
Days are long
Walls close in
The way we see
Doesn't seem so clear
Souls get rattled
We don't have to fly
Let's just stay here
Please hold me
Tight

April love
Come softly
Mind
Is a wildfire
Come take me
I'm spinning stars
And hollow days
April love
Come softly
The sky
Is still shining
But there is nothing
To see
But my heart
Still races
Every time
I say your name

If this is isolation
Give me
More of it
For once
My blood
Is calm
For once
I can rest on needles
And not feel hurt
I awoke in sun
And I had
Blue sky
Dreams

I hope
This time
"I love you"
Becomes more easy
I hope
When we look at
The humans we love
Our eyes
Recognize a galaxy
No more sinking to
The bottom of the ocean
We can say
What we feel

One day we'll get
Back out there
And the way
We hug
The people we love
Will change

Honey
If you and I
Can't go out
And look at the stars
And the way we sleep
In the night
Let's draw them on the ceiling
We'll stay in
Make our universe
A home

Her hands
Felt
Like lost time
She was
A past life
And a sea
Of rain

In my blood
I feel you
You move me
Like a
Cherry blossom tree
Your lips are striking

Of all
The moons
You are
My favorite
And despite
All
The light
You also see
All
My trouble

I love you
When there is no sound
And all we hear is ourselves
How you see
My soul
So hopelessly
Thin
And I see
Your eyes
How they have carried
Many lives
It is hard being human
When we are nothing
But walking
Stories

I never wanted
Power
I just wanted
To feel
I can't lead
Nobody else
Because, most the time
My own soul
Runs in
Every direction

The lights
Haven't been
This alive
In awhile
The glow of you
Is honey
In the night

And
It's in my fingertips
It's in
Those impossible nights
That made me
Catch fire
From the way
I traced I love you
In the palm
Of your hand

I was never
Attracted to gold
I dig wild colors
And when
I look at you
That's all
I see

It felt
Like
The first time
I saw her
Hell had risen
I slept in ashes
And awoke in fire
It felt
Like
The first time
I heard her
The sky lowered
I kissed
The clouds

The wind
Isn't so steady
And everything
We balance
Eventually
Will become
Our skin
So rip me away
My life never fit
In a suitcase
If I am healing
Let me heal
If I am falling
Let me grow

Sunflower dreams
And huckleberry
Eyes
Honey, you shake me
Winter
Hammers down
The cold
Honey, you move me
Your love
Grabs me
By the throat

All the flowers
Couldn't be you
And lord knows
The wind
Doesn't strike me
The way
A heartbeat
Does
I've been knocked
Off my feet
The second
I heard your voice

I thought
Of you
And heard
The sea
I saw you
And felt
Hurricanes

I was attracted
To what she
Wasn't
Never flashy
She moved
Quietly
Through crowds

Cut me open
Just don't let
Everything
I am not
Scare you
You see
I have spent
A lot of time
With my shadows
We can't only be the sun
When we all drip
Trouble
One way
Or the other

I'll love you
Inside this weariness
Where every door
Has slammed shut
And think of me
How I never
Lost sight
Of the monsters
You embraced
Just by saying
My name

And I
Will
Throw away
All the nails
I've kept
I can't bear
To fix
Myself anymore
I am
A crowd
That turns into
A riot

Sometimes
What I hold
In my hand
Isn't always good
But I will share
What I am with you
Quiet
Like a graveyard
Loud
As a train

My heart, my soul
Are not lovers
They are black ice
And I can't see
What is ahead
Sometimes
I am so numb
I don't feel
The crash

Grab a hold
Of me
I feel
You
In my blood
Grab a hold
Of me
Your touch
Shakes me
Like a storm

I spent
All this time
Loving
While my own pieces
Fell to the floor
And every time
It became harder
To pick up
What I am

We were lovers
That was enough
We drank
Good coffee
And that turned us on
Even more
If anything
Made sense
It was mornings
We weren't alone

It wasn't just sparks
It was like walking
Into
The ocean
Sometimes a
Heartbeat
Can cure you
The same way
Saltwater
Can

Silhouette of colors
You are haze
Made of the skies
And I have
Already
Fallen
You've already
Fucked me
With your
Eyes

You looked
Into my hands
And saw how
I've held the wrong people
To love somebody
Is to see
Cuts
Not everyone
Can see

I count to 10
And bite my nails
No air feels safe
Whispering has heard
All failures
I want to scream
So the power of my voice
Can eat away all the worry
This is how
It heals
This is how
It bleeds

She has
Those cannabis eyes
This higher atmosphere
Her love is
Flowers and daggers
I am calm
I am haunted

It's 2:39 am and I love you
It's empty darkness outside
But I still feel
Every light
Honey, I once said
"This life does not
Need to be chained"
You whispered
"How can I fight your demons
When I got mine?"

And if there
Was ever
A time
To go waist deep
Into chaos
It is now
Half of me
Is breathing
The other half
Is lost
In the sea

This was
Cosmic foreplay
Her neck
A meadow
For my lips
Her skin is
Honey
In my hands

My body
Has fed
On the scars
I have
My teeth
Have tore enough
Off the bone
The years
Have loved me
Anyway
I am okay being
Worn

The ocean
Ran through
My bones
You crashed into me
You were water
And I was
Hopelessly
Devoted
To the way
My soul froze
When it saw
Yours

Nothing
Felt right
Everything
Was achy
But more alive
Than it's ever been
This was hostile fire
I couldn't walk away

It's like
She can read
The pain
In me
My flesh
Carry words
Only she
Can see

Sweet like
Strawberry honey
And brave
Like a dandelion
You
Woman
Of this earth
You are
A sunburst
In the
Quiet

The sky
Tore open
All the years
Fell into
My hands
I have
Loved you
When time has stopped
And I have loved you
When every minute
Was fire
In my
Blood

The night is howling
Wind is shaking
You are
Driving
Me mad
Glow of summer
With a gloomy autumn
You're sharp knives
And winter air

I looked myself
In the mirror
On new years day
And I said
Very firmly
"Stay"
People will run away
But, goddamnit
I am staying here

On days
When sunshine
Drowns
I'll keep going
Through
The dark
Maybe
I will breathe
Better
Once this burden
Is off
Of me
Or maybe I will
Say
That carrying
Your own poison
Is sometimes
The remedy

Maybe the highways
Inside me
Have always
Lead to this
Maybe I remember
Burning bridges
While I was busy
Drowning
You see
I can destroy myself
And die happy

Help me
Understand
The waves
That are inside me
Help me
Understand
Why these oceans
Sink me
And i'm on the floor
I'm cursing at the walls
And i'm on the floor
Tearing at my sins
And i'm on the floor
I'm on the floor

The weight
Of my life
Is beginning to
Knock me over
It's how I love
With my heart
On the outside
And all these damn wounds
It's how I breathe
Believing that even
With endless flaws
I can make someone happy

If what I feel
Is too heavy
For my bones
Let it crush me
Because I have loved
You
All these years
I would rather
Get poisoned from flowers
Than be cut by diamonds

I guess it's those moments
When you feel alive
That woman has rain
In her eyes
If this is a flood
I will gladly sink
If we have to find ourselves
I will gladly wait

Take this
Shakiness
From me
Take this heart
That loves
Too much
Out of my body
Let me give you
Part of me
And maybe you can feel
In your hands
What it's like to
Die a thousand
Times

And if
I shatter
I will
Remind you
Even these
Fragments
Can cut
Moments of my life
Are hard
To touch

Hey sarasota
Set me free
I'm here in chains
Still attached
To all these things
Questions linger
Still afraid to finally sleep
Oh sarasota
Set me free
My heart beats
Too wild these days
A sea of feelings
My footsteps are trouble
Sarasota
Set me free

I am
Walking rain
I guess sorrow
Never stays
In one place
You are fire
In the sea
I guess the waves
Could never
Really handle
Your flames
So grab a match
Let's douse the past
With gasoline

She looks like
Sunflowers
In the night
And her eyes
They have never
Been so bright
Forget the rivers
She's all seven seas
Oh, she looks
Like sunflowers
In the night
Let's pack our empty backpacks
Throw in some t-shirts
And some jeans
Let's pack our empty backpacks
And we'll be sunflowers
In the night
Yes, we'll be sunflowers
In the night

Every road
Has seen me
Crawl
Maybe it was from
All those years
Falling in ditches
You see, life did not
Beat me up
I broke my own heart
But what a great
Fucking feeling it is
To now walk around
With lyrics of my life
Written in my skin

I felt it
Through my
Fingertips
This vibe
Of a woman
It has been a blessing
To be touched by warmth
Because lord knows
I have died under
The night sky
Many times

I just felt
Like crying
So I did
Time can't help
My eyes
Feel less empty
I am okay carrying
Around
Life and loss
Moments they were
Never prepared for
And moments I was never
Prepared for

Dazzling lights
Wintry hearts
I'll sit with you
In the cold
Nights are long
It's hard
To breathe
Sit with me
In the cold
Coffee breath
Wild laughs
Sleepy eyes
Full like the moon

If you said
This was
A dream
I would
Collapse into these sheets
Fall asleep
Just to see you
If you said
Time was dead
I would rise
And break the clocks
Those eyes
Tell me exactly
Where I am going

The cold air
Was striking
I never kept
A journal
People probably saw
Ink
Dripping
Off my skin
Words have
Always
Won
The war

I see you
In many ways
I see you
In water
Because of how
You can
Quiet me
The years
Fall off
I don't carry
Anything

My heart
My blood
The nights
They've endured
My eyes
My soul
Still feel
Every word
My hands
My words
Got me jittery
Like the moon

I have buried
Myself
In the stars
And I will
Walk with you
Through the dark

We can
Chase down shadows
And live among
The flowers
Be my dark
I will
Love you
Be my sun
I will
Love you

I love you
And it is written
In my life

Maybe
Just maybe
These vulnerable
Heartbeats hurt me
But all
I know
Is that I love you
All I know
Is that
I love
You

Breathe in the days
With me
Maybe we can get lost
In some little logging town
For a few nights
Drink our coffee
Under trees
I guess we all are
Longing for the normalcy
Of peacetime life
But I also want a gamble
And honey
If we lose
Who says we can't
Roll the dice
Again

I read somewhere
You have about
30-35 minutes
After sunset
Before darkness hits
And in those heavy minutes
I love you the same
I love you in beautiful
Brightness
And every goddamn second
You sink into the cold

When we make it
To the pacific
Let's not
Put these days
On hold
Let's tear open
Every struggle
And breathe
The salty air
When we make it
To the pacific
I hope we stare into
The sea
And realize
We are tides
This
Is the pull
Of moon
And sun
We rise
We fall

If this is
Fire
I will live
In
The ashes
If this is
Water
Let all that I am
Swim with my demons
If every trouble
Finds me
I can't hush it away
I can build houses
While still being
Broken

You are winter
Snow shimmers
In shadows
You are autumn
Chance of rain
A damn book
In those eyes
You are summer
Mountains
And lakes
Stars
Of the milky way
You are spring
Cherry blossom lips
New life
Is born in me
Just by hearing
Your name

What I see
Is you
I am falling
And your eyes
Caught me
I am breathing
And my hell
Is buried

Fireflies
And butterflies
Highways of the soul
Hard as nails
Tender bones
We're just well worn
Summer nights
Winter skies
I'll adore you
Just the same
And when I fall
Shed this skin
You are still a part
Of me

My bones
Have never been my own
They were my father's
They were my mother's
But hope
Has always been
Your eyes
My heart
Feels buried
In the sea
Your laugh
Is like a summer evening
Sunset colors and ice cream

Lonely
Getting lost
Off trails
Set by
My own feet
I'll find me
I'm wrong
Bloody and dirty
Angry
Chasing my shadows
In dreams
Chasing these shadows
In dreams

My mind
Is a jittery
Mess
But I am not
Only darkness
I am also
Light
And I can cover
You
In warmth
Even when I am
Losing
Every war inside
Love your pieces
And never try
To put them
Back together

Your face
Is history
My eyes have
Felt
You
Through years
You have heard me
In broken ways
Even my misery screams
The daylight burns
The sidewalks
Sink

Morning
Is near
And you are
Shining
And beautiful
The sunrise
Bows to your silence
Heavy hands I carry
I'll hold you tight
Heavy hands I carry
I'll hold you
Tight

If I am cracking
Please don't be afraid
Of what spills out
Any direction
Has felt too heavy
I need to breathe
With the water
Because heaven knows
I have too much in me already

I see you
In water
How you
Silence
My screams
I see you
In fire
How you
Rage
And shimmer
In
The night

Why hold
The sunrise
I feel
Her fire
In my bones
Why want jewelry
The shine
Of her
Is in my eyes

I love you
In uneven ways
My heart
Is pulling
Every beginning
Higher
The thought of you
Keeps my feet
On the ground
It is okay
To see me this way
Souls are just
Jagged

The air feels
Alone
All I remember
Is that minutes
Got me into hours
And every second
I stood bleeding
Time hears
Your wounds
More than
People

If autumn
Could speak
She would say
I scatter and fall
Just like
The leaves
When it feels
Like I am holding
Days in my hands
And nights
On my back
She loves me
Anyway

Sun and darkness
Has always
Been now
If silence picks
A room
Laughter
Can still
Fill a house
Wild like the rivers
Haunting
Like the trees

Every star
Is
On fire
And you
Are
Rivers
And
Lakes
And
Sandcastle hearts
My eyes
Are full
The sight of you
Keeps me
Warm

It matters to me
The way my heart
Can be both
Waves
And the rain
I sink
I'll float
Head
Below water
Still stepping
In puddles

I have enough
Miles
In me
Want to be in the sand
And feel the sea
I have enough trouble
In me
Finally ran out of screams
My voice is shot
Sometimes
Bleeding felt
Like a luxury

Things
Are no longer
Resting inside
I found it easy
To get off what was
Bruising me beyond my
Soul
I don't regret
The many sunsets
I was tangled
And crooked
To the core

Pain can be
Scraped off of me
With a knife
But I still love you
My demons were never
Hard to find
They roam
In plain sight
What I feel is
Not just wildflower blue
Sometimes the color
Of hurt
Is hard to see

Star breeze
Sea
Winds of burden
Keep trippin' me
In the streets
Oh, rip these veins
Tear these sheets
Winds of burden
Keep trippin' me
In the streets

Maybe I can
Tell you
What I felt
It was wounds closing up
All the nails fell out
Of me
She is the sun
And I am no longer
In the
Dark

I can't exactly
Say
What is wrong with me
Sometimes flowers
Are disguised as agony
Maybe the night sky
Can look through me
Just a man
With his heart
In his hands

I am brave days
And uncertain warmth
You see
I can be the sun
And still feel every mountain
Inside me crumbling
I won't live in chains
I won't live in chains

Step aside heavy blues
Weighing me down too long
Run away heavy heart
Bring me back
My name
Step aside heavy blues
She is beaming like the sun
Run away heavy heart
Days are worth
The wait

And maybe I love you
The dam is shattering
Oh I am running free
Maybe I see you
You're shades of different times
With hippie in your blood
And those gatsby party vibes

Throw your love
In the sea
Let it sink me
Baby
Let it sink me
Throw your love
In the waves
Throw your love
In the waves
Let it sweep me
Honey
Let it sweep me

Strawberry haze
And your sunshine
Eyes
How can I look away?
What a wonderful
Surprise
Amidst wildflower
Daydreams
To meet you here

It's forever
And
A day
It's the sky
It's the breeze
Heavy rainfall
In the morning
And the warmth of you
In winter
It's forever
And a
Day

Oh, oh oh oh
Now, I want to sit
With her for hours
Laugh until late
The AM will hound us
Now, I want to swim
In her oceans
My head above water
And if I sink
I know she is near me
Inhale all her currents
Campfire and ocean waves

And if
My bones
Break
Please know
It was from
The
Rumblings of
My heart
And this ocean
I call a soul

When shadows
Reach out
To grab you
Remember that
Happiness
Is
The way
You're kidnapped
By the dark
And rescued
By
Your heart

You love me
All through
These troubling
Days
So slip off
That burden
You're okay
Because you've seen me
And i've seen you
i'll love you
All through
These
Troubling days

We hooked up
I felt
Nothing
We argued
I felt
Everything
That's
What it was
Ignoring attachment
And carrying it
With us anyway

The days
Will grow
And I will love you
The years will age
And I will love you

I am spinning
And sinking
And loving
I am a losing grip
Tumbling far
That's why
I feel the mess
But never
The fall

Stand with me
Below
The lights
When darkness keeps me awake
And I need a friend
Stand with me
Below
The lights
I can count
My troubles
And all the reasons
I love you
So i'll take all my sorrows
I'll hold on to
The warmth
That is you
Stand with me
Below
The lights

I love you today
And yesterday
And tomorrow
I'll love you quietly
And loudly
In the rain
In the fire

www.ingramcontent.com/pod-product-compliance
Ingram Content Group UK Ltd.
Pitfield, Milton Keynes, MK11 3LW, UK
UKHW012254290726
14090UKWH00016B/642

9 780578 724706